magic I

sepi

Copyright © 2017 by sepi

www.infinityinfinity.org

ISBN-13: 978-1-942500-37-7
ISBN-10: 942500-37-7

Published by Boulevard Books
www.BoulevardBooks.org

to everyone, once a little one. dedicating this one to you.

here we are, I to I.

will you keep the secret that everyone knows?

the one of the world, the magic I

is all of one point.

no sun, no sky.
no stars to fall, no birds to fly.

simply nothing, as magic I.

who am I?

this magic I.

I am the point of every eye.

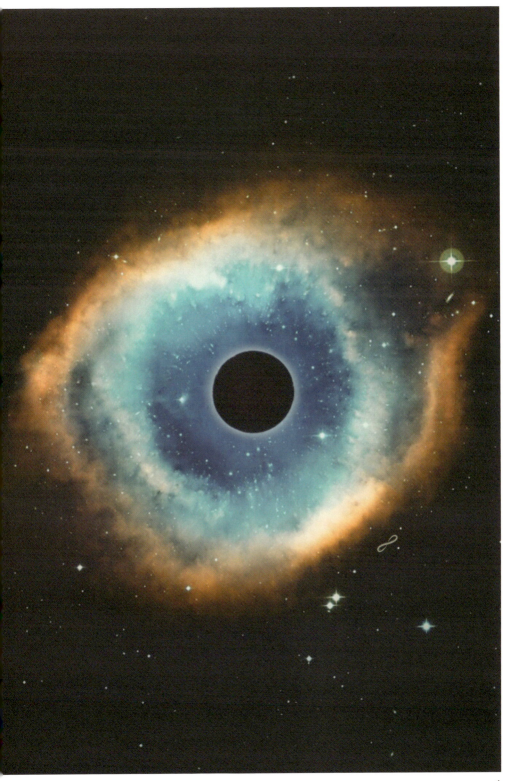

I am as I see

the stars, the skies,
creating the world as it follows my eyes.
and with every heartbeat, the light flows by.

simply nothing as magic I.

I am as I am.
no over,
no under.
no inside,
no outside.
no limit,
no number.

nothing to be added
and nothing removed.
no beginning,
no ending.
not parting.
not glued.

zero is all
and especially not empty.
all I am is fully whole,
all I am right here is plenty.

and there is nothing
            to do
            to be
        who I am.

nothing and all
highs and lows that I swam,
all the blue of all the sky and
all the ocean
I am.

forever I live,
forever I fly
in circles, in circles
to rainbow the sky,
to star
what I see
hello and goodbye to the
sunlight to moonbeams,
all shine from my eyes.

all I am here is magic I.

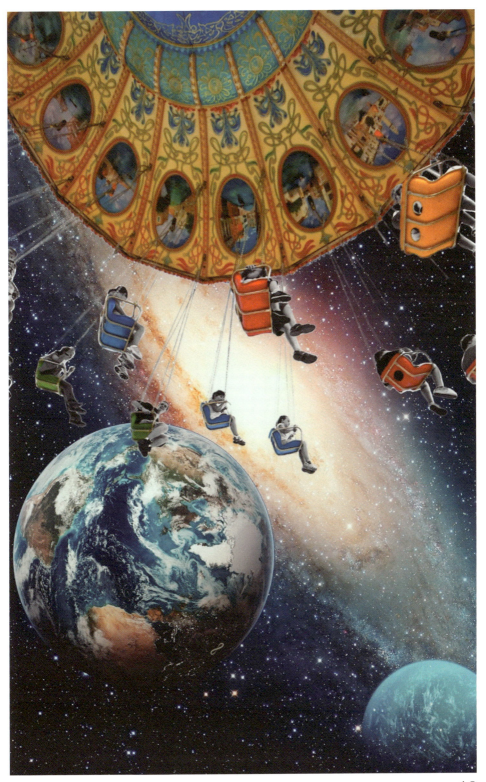

nothing needs not
dream or seem to be,
nothing needs not
appear to see.

zero is no
thing, a magical show,
everything flows from nothing,
so possibly so.

I am nothing and every, as magic I.

zero is naked
being nothing to hide.
zero flows fully
as the wind and the tide.

that follow each other
growing bigger and wide,
the circles flow bigger
with smallers inside
that wish to catch up
after all as they've tried.

I am nothing and every, as magic I.

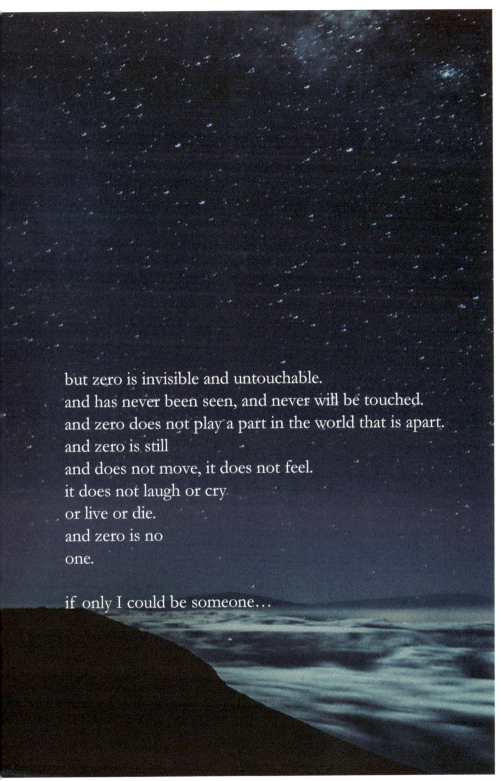

but zero is invisible and untouchable.
and has never been seen, and never will be touched.
and zero does not play a part in the world that is apart.
and zero is still
and does not move, it does not feel.
it does not laugh or cry
or live or die.
and zero is no
one.

if only I could be someone…

I am a little one.

me me me

        me me

me me

yes, I am special, no one is like me.

me, I will
always be free
to be.

me, I can be, changing thoughts in my mind,
playing hide-and-seek as me, every lifetime to find.
and thoughts of me circle, rewind and unwind.

me, I can see, as magic I.

as I put on a face and chase phase after a phase

or put on a hat and play this or that.

the mind moves the heart,
emotions wave as they flow
in motions, in moments,
they come and they go.

me, I can see, as magic I.

but me is my colors and the things that I do.
the light changes colors,
green, violet, and blue,
and red, and orange, and yellow, too.

I am not wherever I may go
or places I have been.
I am never without everything,
my heart is here within.

I can think of me as
more than,
better than, or
different than
the rest.
the me that is becoming
is always longing to be
best.

no one is me, yes, this is true,
but I am far beyond far the things that I do.
I do things in circles,
and I am still
here when they're through.
the one that is still
is the one that is true.

the one I am is more than me.
the one I am is myself, the ever-be.

the ever-so here, the closer than near.
the center of love, as myself, there's no fear.

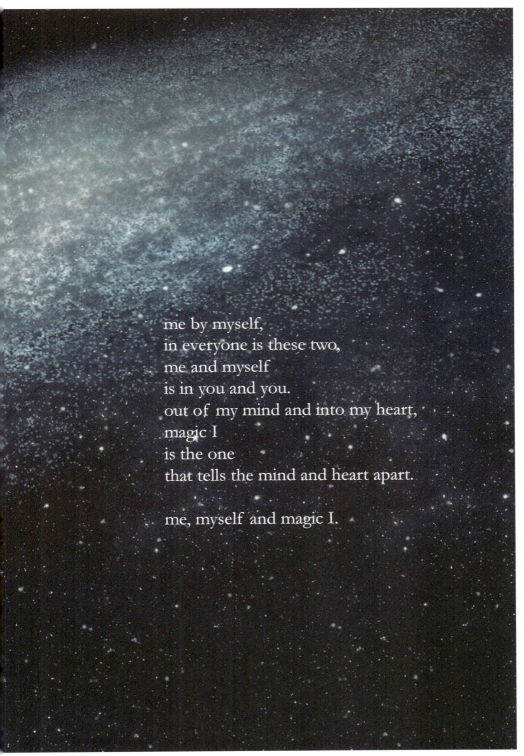

me by myself,
in everyone is these two,
me and myself
is in you and you.
out of my mind and into my heart,
magic I
is the one
that tells the mind and heart apart.

me, myself and magic I.

these mindstrings pull heartstrings,
tied for magic I to choose,
in this otherworld of others
pretenders play as twos.

they pretend to lose the magic I,
mindbright shadowed and confused,
pretending heartlight can be covered,
endless games of win or lose.

and things, and thinks, and feels get tangled
in twists, and turns and knots.
but magic I sees between the ever-is and the is-nots.

the twos of this play
move in mind and still in heart.
magic I is here to part the sea
and spell the mind as one with heart.

and true magicians keep the secret
that everyone knows,
illusions of the mind play tricks
of how this story goes…

the one of the world,
the magic I
is all of one point
and all of the sky,
the minds that fall,
the hearts that fly…

love is who I am,

magic I to I.

about the author

sepi is presently and poetically living in new york city. with love of artistic expression from an early age, she is sharing her poetry and illustrations with the world. sepi's writing is rooted in the harmony of oneness and seeking of universal truth. her career as a high school science teacher gifts her with the unique opportunity of presenting the chemistry and physics of life in a philosophically relatable way. with an educational background in psychology and medical biology, along with a masters of arts in teaching, she infuses her work with deep insight as she carefully shines light to unify the physical, psychological and spiritual energies in the hearts of her readers.

join sepi on the path of love, self-discovery and unity consciousness on social media @sepinfinity

www.infinityinfinity.org

CPSIA information can be obtained at www.ICGtesting.com
Printed in the USA
BVIW12n2225281217
503954BV00006B/8